The Little of Mark Making

The meaningful marks of young children

Written by Sam Goodman
and Elaine Massey

Photographs by Sam Goodman

LITTLE BOOKS WITH BIG **IDEAS**

Published 2009 by A&C Black Publishers Limited
36 Soho Square, London W1D 3QY
www.acblack.com

ISBN 978-1-9060-2909-8

First published in the UK by Featherstone Education, 2007

Printed in Great Britain by Latimer Trend & Company Limited.

This book is produced using paper that is made from wood grown in
managed, sustainable forests. It is natural, renewable and recyclable.

The logging and manufacturing processes conform to the environmental
regulations of the country of origin.

inge of titles
)lack.com

Contents

Introduction

Mark making isn't just about pencils or paint on paper. You can make a mark with any part of your body, on any type of surface. You can use kitchen implements, tools, material, toys the list is as long as your imagination. Mark making should be fun! It should be an exploration of different materials, different media, and an opportunity for children to see how they can make marks. The journey towards writing begins in making marks, and early marks happen when fingers drizzle in spilt food, making finger patterns before the food is wiped away; and as we offer access to a wide range of materials we should be praising and recognising every child's mark making efforts.

Children must see adults writing, and we should all model good practice for them. We should offer opportunities to write wherever possible, but know that writing begins by making marks and not by producing letters.

Mark making for children should be about the enjoyment of creating, rather than working on empty, adult directed tasks or goals which can, and often do, lead to frustration and lack of engagement.

Before any child is ready to make marks confidently they need many opportunities to refine both their gross motor and fine motor skills through movement.

What are fine motor skills?

These are the skills a child needs to manipulate and control a range of tools and materials. They are the small, precise thumb, finger, hand and wrist movements used in coordination with the eyes.

Fine motor skills are used when **grasping** (using crayons, pencils, paint brushes, glue sticks, blocks etc.), **manipulating** (plasticine, play dough, clay, scissors etc.) and **developing hand eye co-ordination** (in mark making, writing, cutting, threading, moving a computer cursor, throwing and catching etc.).

Developing fine motor skills, coordination and dexterity are all vital for learning to write but children should have developed the necessary strength and dexterity in their hands and fingers before being asked to manipulate a pencil on paper. The more children use their hands the finer the movements become. Children need lots of opportunities and encouragement to explore mark making and creating patterns. Gradually their experiences on paper, clay, fabrics, foam etc. will take on a more writing-like quality and they will start to ascribe meaning to their marks. Of course, this stage must be achieved before children can ascribe meaning to the marks made by others!

Some activities for developing fine motor skills:

- ▶ making puzzles – start with simple 'peg' puzzles with few pieces, progressing to more pieces as skill improves;
- ▶ playing with blocks – start off with larger blocks and progress to smaller bricks;
- ▶ painting – offer a selection of brushes from very fine to large decorators' brushes;
- ▶ drawing with crayons/pencils/chalks and charcoal;
- ▶ exploring play dough/clay/Plasticine – with a variety of equipment such as rollers and shape cutters;
- ▶ cutting malleable materials with scissors and plastic knives, and molding and rolling it;
- ▶ making marks in materials with a selection of of tools – cutlery, sticks, coins, keys, combs, pencils etc;
- ▶ threading – with beads and pasta or through trellis with wool, ribbon, tape, string;
- ▶ lacing and sewing activities;
- ▶ using pegs and pegboards;
- ▶ experimenting with stamping sets – make your own by carving shapes into potatoes or polystyrene;
- ▶ tearing and scrunching newspaper (a super strength builder);
- ▶ cutting and snipping paper with scissors;
- ▶ using tweezers and tongs – to pick up small things;
- ▶ using hammers, saws, screwdrivers;
- ▶ peeling and sticking stickers;
- ▶ using eye droppers, pipettes, turkey basters to pick up liquids;
- ▶ using clothes pegs to hang washing out, numbers on number lines, making shelters and dens;
- ▶ playing finger games (Two Little Dicky Birds, Round and Round the Garden);
- ▶ using role play cash registers, mobile phones, telephones;
- ▶ looking at books, magazines, comics (with plenty of page turning);
- ▶ buttoning and zipping clothes and doll's clothes;
- ▶ playing musical instruments;
- ▶ using Tap Tap (nails and cork boards) or Fuzzy Felt pictures;
- ▶ using magnets to make pictures and faces;
- ▶ playing with with all sorts of small world play animals and people in sand, water, brick play;
- ▶ cooking – chopping, slicing, grating, mixing, pouring, spreading.

Development Stages and Early Learning Goals for fine motor skills

- ▶ Engage in activities requiring hand - eye co-ordination.
- ▶ Use one handed tools and equipment.
- ▶ Demonstrate increasing skill and control in the use of mark making.
- ▶ Manipulate materials and objects by picking up, releasing, arranging, threading them.
- ▶ Combine and repeat a range of movements.
- ▶ Move with control and co-ordination.
- ▶ Understand that tools have to be used safely.
- ▶ Explore malleable materials by patting, poking, squeezing, pinching and twisting them.
- ▶ Manipulate materials to achieve a planned effect.
- ▶ Use simple tools to effect changes to the materials.
- ▶ Handle tools and malleable materials safely and with increasing control.
- ▶ Show a clear and consistent preference for the right or left hand.

Using their bodies and developing gross motor skills

Children need to feel confident to explore mark making and refine their physical development throughout their environment. Although the body is still when we make marks, draw or write, the muscles, nerves, thoughts and feelings are active all of the time, and tasks requiring fine motor skills, such as writing, painting, threading and arranging, all involve larger and stronger muscles. Before being able to hold and manipulate a pencil, paintbrush or other tools, children need to be in control of the muscles in their hands, bodies and eyes. They develop this control in many ways through exercise, play, music and movement and that is why it is vital that they are given every opportunity to be physically active. Children need to run, jump, roll, crawl, walk, skip, dance, slide, hop, kick, throw, catch, pedal, swing, climb and balance to help develop control over their muscles. Later learning will be easier if children have had lots of practice using both sides of their body.

Some activities where children can use both sides of the body:

- ▶ making foam patterns;
- ▶ finger sticker dancing: decorating the end of each finger with a sticker (both hands) and watching their fingers dance to music in a large mirror;
- ▶ ribbon/scarf/streamer dancing: start with one hand and progress to both, and explore the ways in which they can be moved;
- ▶ holding objects in each hand and moving arms up and down and from side to side;
- ▶ listening to music and dancing to develop rhythm and flow in their movements;
- ▶ dressing up: pulling clothes on and off using both hands;
- ▶ moving prams, wheelbarrows, trolleys, carts, toy lawn mowers, bikes, scooters etc;
- ▶ playing musical instruments: drums (both hands for tapping and holding drumsticks), piano, xylophones, maracas, bells, tambourines, cymbals etc;
- ▶ specialised movement schemes such as Jabadeo, Activate and Write Dance (see page 95);
- ▶ Brain Gym movements (see page 95).

What are gross motor skills?

Usually, large muscles develop before smaller ones, so gross motor development can be seen as the foundation for developing skills in other areas such as fine motor skills. Children learn new gross motor skills by practising them until the skill is mastered, so opportunities must be given for children to have time to try and then try again and again. Most gross motor skills are learned in early childhood, and good gross motor skills are absolutely essential!

These skills include:

- ▶ balance;
- ▶ body awareness;
- ▶ major muscle co-ordination;
- ▶ crossing of the mid line;
- ▶ laterality (awareness and use of of both sides of their bodies and a dominance of one hand, foot or eye in some activities);
- ▶ spatial orientation (body awareness in relation to others and to objects).

The body develops from large movements such as control of the trunk, arms and legs, to small isolated movements that include the hands and fingers.

Without reasonable gross motor control it can be very difficult for children to move on to developing the fine motor skills, which enable them to thread beads, use the pincer grasp (thumb and forefinger), to cut, and later to develop a confident handwriting style. These large movements are often made naturally during play outdoors in activities such as:

walking	jumping	catching balls
running	hopping	kicking balls
galloping	climbing	throwing balls
crawling	skipping	ball games.

Children who have constant access to the outdoors in their settings and at home will develop and be able to practise their gross motor skills if given the time to do so. Offer them opportunities to help with gardening, and other outside chores at home. Let children climb, run, jump and scramble safely but adventurously.

A child's ability to perform motor skills depends on factors including muscle strength and coordination and flexibility. Sometimes problems with low muscle tone and balance can also affect the development of gross motor skills, and at times physical therapy may be needed to help advance a child's skills.

Some activities for developing gross motor skills:

- using large equipment, ie frames for climbing and swinging, at home or at the park;
- running – lots of outdoor opportunities to run and to change speed and direction;
- hopping – can help to develop balance skills;
- ball play of all types with big and small balls;
- games with bats.... try with a balloon first rather than a ball;
- giving opportunities to explore and enjoy movement;
- movement matching and copying games;
- pushing and pulling large wheeled toys;
- using safe stools, step stools and ladders in play;
- stirring and mixing cakes and puddings;
- ramps/bridges with vehicles;
- using the interactive white board (IWB);
- crawling through tunnels;
- large weaving – possibly outdoors on your fence;
- rolling playdough;
- rolling cable reels and barrels;
- using pulleys with buckets attached;
- building large construction indoors and outdoors.

Some activities for developing gross motor skills:

- Manage body to create intended movements.
- Combine and repeat a range of movements.
- Move with control and co-ordination.
- Construct with large materials such as cartons, long lengths of fabric and planks.
- Use increasing control over an object by touching, pushing, patting, throwing, catching or kicking it.
- Use a wide range of small and large equipment.
- Use one handed tools and equipment.

Drawing

We sometimes forget the power of drawing and it becomes a time filler, rather than the powerful expressive activity it should be.

What you need

- ▶ paper and card of different colours, sizes, shapes and weights
- ▶ free access to a range of drawing equipment – pencils, crayons, felt pens (thick and fine), highlighter pens, chalk, oil pastels, soft pastels, graphite sticks, charcoal etc.

What you do

Preparation

▶ Look carefully at your room and the garden and see how many opportunities you can provide for children to draw. Do you have seats, cushions, mats and clipboards outside? Do you have plenty of space for children to draw on all sorts of surfaces indoors? Do you inspire their drawings by giving them plenty of interesting subjects, activities and objects to draw? Do you value their work by providing spaces where they can display their own pictures? Do you look at books, go to museums, look at drawing on TV and in stories? Do you draw yourself and invite artists to visit your setting?

Exploration

▶ Make sure children have the time, space and equipment to experiment with all sorts of drawings and tools. Sit with them as they work and talk about what they are doing. Provide objects for them to draw if they wish. Let them talk to the group about drawing, not just about writing.

An extension:

Offer new surfaces for drawing on – acetate, whiteboards, empty cardboard boxes, hardboard and plywood, coloured and textured papers, including art papers such as cartridge and watercolour paper.

Ready for more...

▶ Expand the range of mark making out of doors by using mud, drawing in sand, using chalk on walls and paths, putting up big blackboards and huge sheets of paper or card, even snow!

▶ Offer children their own sketchbooks (at least A4 size) and let them use these whenever they want to.

▶ Offer fine black markers and smooth cartridge paper for detailed drawings.

▶ Make close observational drawing a regular feature of your week by providing interesting objects to draw – natural and seasonal things such as a sunflower seed head, snowdrops, or a pumpkin – or a bike, a musical instrument, a machine, a holiday souvenir, a beautiful shell or a Christmas ornament.

Painting

Painting is another standard activity in early years settings, but it is often boring and unchanging. Let some fresh ideas brighten up your painting places.

What you need

- as many different sorts of paint as you can find - poster, powder, acrylic, oil, watercolour, enamel, fabric, chroma and emulsion
- a wide range of surfaces to paint on
- lots of different sorts of brushes and markers; containers for mixing
- stuff to mix with paint – glue, sand, mud, glitter, paste, flour

What you do

Preparation

▶ Make sure children have aprons or other protective clothing that is easy to put on and doesn't get in the way as they paint.
Have clear guidance on the ways children work – how much independence they have in making and mixing paint, the sorts of containers, mark makers and surfaces they can use, the places they can work. Be as flexible as you can, talk about rules and make sure you are clear about boundaries.

Exploration

▶ Give daily opportunities for using paint in different ways, as child-initiated activities and in more adult directed times.

▶ Spend time with the children as they paint, talking about what they are doing and valuing the work they produce.

Some extensions:

1. Suggest some collaborative painting activities on big surfaces indoors and outside, on floors, walls, big sheets of card, paper, shower curtains, bubble wrap, fabrics.

2. Sometimes offer a limited colour range of paint or some unusually shaped pieces of paper.

Ready for more...

▶ Screw some wooden battens to the walls outside, so you can fix paper to them with pins for outdoor painting.

▶ Offer hand sprayers and thin paint for painting on big sheets of shower curtains.

▶ Paint standing up, or lying down.

▶ Offer some inspiration by looking at paintings in books, visiting museums and galleries, looking on the Internet, inviting local artists to visit, pinning up posters and postcards.

▶ Give some display space for a gallery where children can display their paintings and drawings – and photos of the ones that are too big or were painted on floors or walls.

▶ Have a go youself, so children know that grown-ups paint too!

More drawing and painting

More ideas for drawing and painting to try in your setting. Try:

Using card from big cartons for drawing on vertical surfaces

Oil pastels · Group drawing · Soft pastels

Observational drawing · Charcoal · Markers

Painting outdoors on big pieces of paper or plastic

Something unusual

All sorts of tools

Colour mixing for shades

A limited colour palette

Paint on leaves and stones

All sorts of surfaces

Giving time for exploration

Indoor water

Making marks with water is fun anywhere! Try these ideas for using water to make marks indoors.

What you need

- ▶ small blackboards
- ▶ cotton buds
- ▶ small cloths and sponges
- ▶ small plastic containers for water

What you do

Preparation
▶ Once you have the blackboards, no preparation is necessary for this activity.

Exploration
▶ Cotton bud painting can be totally independent and child-initiated once you have introduced the idea and put the materials in an available place.
▶ Children will enjoy simply dipping the cotton buds in water and drawing on the boards. Marks and patterns are easily changed or rearranged using a small cloth or sponge.

Some extensions:
1. Make your own blackboards by painting offcuts of wood with blackboard paint.

2. Offer black paper and masking tape so children can stick the paper down to a table themselves for a different sort of water painting.

3. Try covering a whole table with black paper for a group activity.

4. Use a cotton bud in each hand for more fun and development of co-ordination, or use two buds in one hand.

5. Walk wet fingers in a pattern round the surface.

Ready for more...

▶ Offer other small mark makers such as fine paint brushes, little sponge shapes, cut vegetables.

▶ Old, dried out felt pens will often come to new life when dipped in water and used for drawing.

▶ Sponge dabbers (or small pieces of sponge fixed on sticks) will also make interesting marks.

▶ You could also offer small mark making tools outside to extend children's experiences of water painting outdoors.

▶ Make hand prints, draw round your hands, make lines of finger prints with an index finger.

Outdoor water

Children love using water outside, and most settings offer painting with water as a child-initiated activity. Try varying the scale of water painting in your setting!

What you need

▶ an outside tap is ideal for this sort of activity, but a big bucket, bowls or a water tray on the ground will do

▶ brooms, mops and brushes

What you do

Preparation
▶ Collect the materials and tools, and introduce them to the children. Explain the places and areas for the work, and talk about safety with broom handles!

Exploration
▶ This is a totally self-initiated activity, but needs some careful supervision while children get used to using the brushes and mops.

Some extensions:
1. Get some child-sized brooms, mops and brushes, and add these to the adult sized ones. If you get adult-sized tools, you may want to make the handles shorter by sawing them off to about half their length.

2. Add some washing up liquid for bubbly water.

3. Make paths for walking, running or biking through water and making tracks.

4. Use the brushes and mops on walls and doors.

5. Use water, mops and brushes to clean the bikes and other vehicles.

Ready for more...

▶ This activity is great for developing shoulder and upper arm muscles, so encourage both boys and girls to get involved.

▶ Add some watering cans (with and without sprinklers on the ends) for a different water experience.

▶ Encourage children to make faces, letters, names and patterns on the ground with the water. Spin around as the water pours out, make zigzags.

▶ Get some metal or plastic teapots from charity shops and use these for pattern making.

▶ Get a rope or thick cord and dip in water to drag around for marking.

▶ After rain, sweep the puddles, or put on your wellies and walk through the puddles to make tracks, or ride bikes and scooters through the puddles. On fine days, you could make a puddle on purpose!

Outdoor chalkboards

Blackboards are a cheap and reusable mark making surface which children love. Have a chalkboard outside and make it as big as you can fit in the space.

What you need

▶ a large, wall mounted chalkboard
▶ chalks (big pavement chalk and smaller classroom chalk)
▶ decorating rollers, brushes and sponges; containers for water

What you do

Preparation

▶ Little preparation is needed for this everyday activity which children can join and leave at their choice. Just make the board as big as possible – right from the ground to the furthest reaching height of the oldest children.

Exploration

▶ Offer plenty of containers and chalks (perhaps on a trolley or in a basket).

▶ Join in sometimes to give the activity extra interest and credibility, and to give you opportunities to observe and listen.

Some extensions:

1. If you haven't got a chalkboard, use the side of a shed or a wall. Paint this with blackboard paint or just leave it as it is.

2. Encourage the children to use their whole bodies as they reach, stretch, make huge patterns, pictures, circles and lines.

3. Take photos of the work before it disappears.

4. Use a hose or rollers and water to remove chalk pictures when the children have finished.

Ready for more...

▶ Use small decorating rollers, brushes, sponges and water on chalkboards or painted walls.

▶ Offer small chalkboards and chalk as an outdoor activity as well as indoors.

▶ Use up left-over chalk ends by putting them in a zip-lock bag and bashing them with a wooden brick or mallet till they are a powder. Tip the powder into small containers and add a bit of water to make 'chalk paint'. You can use this to paint coloured chalk pictures on walls, fences and paving stones with rollers and brushes.

More water and chalk

More ideas for chalk and water to try in your setting.

Two hands are better than one! Encourage drawing with two chalks, making big marks and circles to help co-ordination.

Small chalkboards outside – same picture, same child, many versions!.

Take easels outside for chalk or water painting.

Chalk on paths and paving stones, walls, sheds or big pieces of wood.

Use coloured chalk on big sheets of paper.

Offer water painting at all times of the year and in all weathers to harness natural energy into enjoyable activities that help with fine motor skills.

Scarves for movement

Buy some chiffon scarves from a market or a charity shop. These will give you lots of fun as the children practise movement and making shapes in the air.

What you need

- chiffon scarves (all sizes) – try charity shops or street markets
- pieces of voile or gauze
- ribbons
- plenty of space

What you do

Preparation
▶ Look at the scarves and ribbons together and talk about how they feel and how they behave in the air when you toss them gently upwards.

Exploration
▶ Give the children plenty of time to explore how the scarves, ribbons and fabrics move. Encourage them to move indoors and outside, tossing and circling independently.

▶ Explore how the objects move when you try to toss them to someone else.

▶ Let the children explore making free movement patterns to music.

Some extensions:
1. Work with a group to explore how the materials move when you make specific moves, such as a circle with your whole arm, a wave up and down, dropping them from a height, running and stopping.

2. How many different ways can you make the scarf move without moving your feet? What happens when you jump? Skip? Twirl? Run?

Ready for more...

▶ As children become more familiar with using scarves and ribbons, use them to practise the shapes for writing – circles (clockwise and anti-clockwise), up and down lines, difficult letters such as 'e' or 'g'.

▶ Use a scarf or ribbon in each hand, or in their 'non-dominant' hand to help with gross and fine movement and hand-eye co-ordination.

▶ Attach ribbons to short sticks or canes and use these as an alternative for moving to music, or rhythm.

Ribbon pictures

Collect ribbons from markets, florists, gift ribbon, and strings for these activities. You could also ask parents and colleagues for contributions.

What you need

▶ long lengths of ribbon
▶ floor or table space

What you do

Preparation

▶ Leave the ribbons where the children can explore them freely during child-initiated learning times.

Exploration

▶ Let the children have plenty of time to explore what the ribbons can do, looking at and feeling the colours, lengths and textures. They may want to move around with the ribbons before using them to make shapes, patterns or pictures on the floor or table.

▶ Take photos and talk with them about what they are doing.

Some extensions:

1. Try some work in pairs or groups, exploring the ribbons.

2. Try making numbers, letters and shapes with the ribbons.

3. Expand the range of ribbons with lace trim, string, wool, laces, rope, twine.

4. Put a layer of white glue in a shallow tray or lid for more permanent pictures, where the children arrange their ribbons and other objects and leave them to dry. Drying takes a bit of time, so be patient! Hang the lids on strings or more ribbon for display.

Ready for more...

▶ Use the ribbons for dancing or movement. You could tie them around children's wrists for dancing indoors and outside on a windy day.

▶ Dip the end of a ribbon in paint and hold the other end for a wavy, wobbly mark maker which encourages concentration and eye/hand co ordination.

▶ Ribbons can help with writing practice! Use them tied to sticks or just in their hands to make letter shapes in the air. Try with one hand or both, or use some of the ideas on the previous page, using ribbons or ribbon sticks instead of scarves.

Conker creations

Natural materials such as conkers, shells, nuts and stones can be used for mark making. They are free and natural resources that every child should experience.

What you need

▶ lots of conkers!
▶ a piece of plain fabric to cover a table or put in a builder's tray

What you do

Preparation

▶ Make sure there is plenty of space for the child or children to explore the materials. Don't make any expectations about what they will do.

▶ Leave these materials for children to explore independently. You could sit with them and talk about what they are doing, but try not to interfere or turn their activity into your activity!

▶ Talk about what they are doing, but don't forget that silence is also encouraging! Take photos to display or talk about what they are doing – this activity is ephemeral, but needs recognition as important and valued work.

Exploration

▶ Let the children have plenty of time to explore what the ribbons can do, looking at and feeling the colours, lengths and textures. They may want to move around with the ribbons before using them to make shapes, patterns or pictures on the floor or table.

▶ Take photos and talk with them about what they are doing.

Some extensions:

1. Expand the space for this sort of activity – the paths and patterns could go anywhere, indoors or outside.

2. Add chalk, felt pens and other mark makers to extend the play.

Ready for more...

▶ Anything natural or man-made can be used for these sorts of mark making experiments, you just need big quantities. Children can use one sort or a mixture, but a single object in abundance and repeated has a real fascination, so get collecting! Try some of these:

Natural materials such as leaves, nuts, sticks, twigs, gravel, shells, feathers, natural or polished pebbles and stones.

Man-made materials such as tops and lids, CDs, packaging materials, buttons, beads, big sequins, glass beads, polystyrene packaging materials, pasta shapes, clothes pegs and big elastic bands.

The essence of this activity is that it is NOT permanent! Or only as permanent as you can make it! The pictures at the end of the book show what happened when a group of children had access to a huge number of CDs.

Sand, sticks and stones

Stones and pebbles are free and sand and lolly sticks are cheap. No setting should be without these flexible and tactile resources.

What you need

- dry silver or 'play' sand
- polished pebbles, lolly sticks or natural sticks
- shallow containers such as builders' trays or plant saucers for sand
- coloured paper, foil and fabric

What you do

Preparation

▶ Line the shallow trays with brightly coloured paper or foil.

▶ Put a shallow layer of sand in the trays. Leave the pebbles in an accessible container. Leave some containers without sand.

Exploration

▶ Leave the trays where children can play with them freely indoors or outside.

▶ Encourage the children to choose whether to use sand, pebbles or both.

Some extensions:

1. Children could use the trays to make patterns or pictures with sand, gravel and pebbles.

2. They could make patterns with their fingers in the sand, so the coloured paper shows through.

3. If they are ready and physically able, encourage the isolation of their forefingers and the use of both hands. This will help with mark making and writing.

Ready for more...

▶ Add some small hand tools, such as brushes, card or plastic sand combs or glue spreaders.

▶ Instead of sand, use porridge oats, glitter, lentils or flour.

▶ Put a big piece of fabric on the floor for a larger version of the activity.

▶ Use a tarpaulin, shower curtain or the flip side of a road mat for a firmer surface.

▶ Make the sand patterns permanent, sprinkle a thin layer of sand on paper, let the children make patterns with their fingers, then spray the marks with a contrasting coloured aerosol spray (adults only, and in a well ventilated area!). Leave the pattern for a moment, then tip any loose sand into the bin. You are left with a relief pattern of the marks made by the children.

Damp sand

Give children both damp and dry sand to explore. They behave quite differently and damp sand has the advantage of holding a shape, mark or texture.

What you need

I will need

▶ damp sand in a sand tray or shallow containers

▶ mark making tools such as rakes, cutlery, cookie cutters, pencils, sticks and twigs, playdough tools, beakers, shells, bowls, sand moulds and rope

What you do

Preparation

▶ Let the children make dry sand damp by sprinkling water on it with a plant spray (this is also good for strengthening hand muscles).

▶ Leave the tools in containers nearby.

Exploration

▶ Give time for free play before getting involved in suggestions or adult direction.

Some extensions:

1. Use the back of a rake or spade, or their hands to pat the sand flat for mark making.

2. Talk about the marks made by the different tools and equipment.

3. Get the children to look for other mark makers at home or in your setting.

4. Look in education supply catalogues for sand rollers, moulds and other markers to extend your collection.

5. Try charity and 'Pound' shops for kitchen implements and other mark makers.

Ready for more...

▶ Look for unusual moulds, such as packaging materials.

▶ Find natural objects such as shells, cones and stones that make interesting prints.

▶ Press rope, string, buttons and coins into the sand.

▶ Use buckets to make sand pies and castles and add patterns with your mark makers.

▶ Make smaller versions by putting damp sand in plastic lids or baking trays and using cocktail sticks, pegs and pencils to make the patterns.

▶ Collect leaves, petals, seeds and twigs to make gardens in the sand. This small scale work all helps with hand control.

Soapy suds

A familiar substance for making marks. Try different kinds and perfumes of washing-up liquid and bubble bath.

What you need

- washing-up liquid or bubble bath
- a large area – table or floor
- an old shower curtain or plastic sheet
- a bucket or washing up bowl
- long handled spoon or whisk for whipping lather

> **SAFETY**
> Check for allergies or use non-allergenic products to be safe.

What you do

Preparation
▶ Add a small amount of water to a generous amount of washing-up liquid in a bucket.

Exploration
▶ Work with the children to whisk the mixture with spoons and wire whisks to create a really thick lather. This will be great fun!

▶ Cover a large table with a plastic sheet or old shower curtain, and spread the mixture on the table top. You could put the tray on the floor instead – indoors or in the garden.

▶ Let the children explore with their fingers and hands.

Some extensions:
1. Show the children how to erase the marks they make by smoothing the foam with the flat of their hands.

2. Take some photos together to talk about later.

3. Encourage the children to use both hands and big movements.

4. Watch for children who can isolate their index finger to refine their marks, and those who can't yet do this.

5. Children could work in pairs to create patterns and marks.

Ready for more...

▶ Offer a little poster paint or ready mixed paint to add to the soap suds. This will colour the foam and enable children to explore color mixing.

▶ Instead of using hands or fingers to make marks provide a selection of tools to use: sticks, a range of paintbrushes, combs, cutlery, stiff strips of card, small garden canes.

▶ Remember this activity can be done indoors or outside.

▶ If you don't have space or a large surface area available you could use a large tray (builders trays will encourage larger mark making than the usual tea tray size) or large chopping boards.

▶ Try using soap flakes instead of washing-up liquid – you'll get a very different experience!

Shaving foam

A cheap and exciting resource, which never loses its appeal – remember to use non-allergenic versions if you have children with sensitive skins or reactions.

What you need

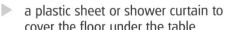

- cans of shaving foam
- a smooth flat surface to work on
- a plastic sheet or shower curtain to cover the floor under the table

> **SAFETY**
> Check for allergies or use non-allergenic products to be safe.

What you do

Preparation

▶ Look at the spray cans together, and talk about safe use. Children can do this activity independently if they have been shown how to do it.

Exploration

▶ Help the children to spray a thick and generous layer of foam over the surface you have chosen.

▶ Leave the children to explore the foam, swirling and shaping it with hands and fingers.

▶ Stay nearby, so you can get involved in the conversations about what the foam does and how it feels.

▶ Don't forget to have a go yourself – this will give a good message about messy play, but don't be tempted to turn it into a letter formation session!

Some extensions:

1. Encourage the children to use both hands and all their fingers. This will help with fine motor development and writing skills.

2. Comment on the marks the children make with their hands and fingers. If they are interested, talk about wavy, zigzag or straight lines in the foam.

3. Encourage and model descriptive language such as 'smooth', 'slimy', 'slippery', 'bubbly', 'marks', 'patterns', 'finger', 'hand', 'palm', 'fist', 'spike', 'lump' and 'flat'.

Ready for more...

▶ Offer tools such as small spades, plastic knives and forks, brushes etc.

▶ Sprinkle glitter on the surface to make it more magical.

▶ Add a squirt of ready mixed paint or sprinkle dry powder paint on the surface. Leave it for the children to incorporate as they work, and stay near as they describe what happens.

▶ Use toy cars to make tracks and patterns.

▶ Try shaving gels –some of these change colour as you use them.

▶ Use bare feet and toes to explore the foam. Have a bowl of water ready for washing afterwards, or do this outside.

Finger printing

Finger painting is a classic activity for free mark making. Provide this permanently for child-initiated times, so children can help themselves to materials they need.

What you need

- ▶ a wipe-clean surface
- ▶ thick paint; simple mark making tools
- ▶ paper for prints

What you do

Preparation

▶ Prepare the paints and put them in suitable containers –
squeezy bottles work well. Offer several colours and the
opportunity to mix shades of these to make new colours.

Exploration

▶ Work with the children as they mix paints and spread them on the surface of a
table with a brush or their hands. To start with, just let them experience the
textures and colours of the paints, making marks and patterns with their fingers
and other marking tools such as card combs, sticks, or sponges.
Explain how to erase their marks with their hands if they want to start again.

Some extensions:

1. Explore taking prints of the patterns and pictures the children make. Help them to
put a piece of paper over their finger painting and smooth it gently with the flat
of their hands. If they press too hard they will squash the painting.

2. Experiment with different colours and types of paper for prints – a contrasting
colour will make the print stand out, a toning colour may make a pleasing effect.
Try printing on foil, on plastic, on polystyrene tiles. Add things to the paint –
sand, detergent, glitter, white glue and talk about the different surfaces and sorts
of paint, and which work best.

Ready for more...

▶ Finger painting is essentially a child-initiated, free activity with no other
purpose than creating a unique design. However, this method can be used
for other sorts of mark making activities. Try these:

▷ Use fingers and finger paint to
record close observations of
flowers, seeds, shoots, leaves –
make prints of these for display.

▷ Make repeating patterns in paint
with fingers and other mark
makers and take prints.

▷ Write letters and words and then
take prints – discuss what has
happened to the letters and why
that might be.

▷ Use a limited palette to make
finger painted backgrounds for
themed displays or to back a board
full of paintings or line drawings.

Paint ball!

This activity needs space, and can be messy, but it is great fun! Cover vulnerable surfaces with a shower curtain or dust sheet.

What you need

I will need

▶ a selection of balls – different sizes, shapes and surfaces – balls for table tennis, tennis, golf, football, rugby, beach games, textured, koosh etc.
▶ paint in shallow trays
▶ large pieces of paper – try wallpaper or lining paper, even newspaper

What you do

Preparation

▶ Find a suitable space indoors or outside, and cover any vulnerable surfaces.

▶ Spread the paper out, and secure the corners if you need to (big stones on the corners work well outside).

▶ Pour some paint into shallow trays and put the balls in a basket or box.

Exploration

▶ Talk the process through with the children, then let them experiment with the activity, dipping the different balls in the paint and rolling them across the paper.

Some extensions:

1. Try different ways of using the balls – dropping, bouncing, pushing as well as rolling.

2. Take photos of the process and the final product.

3. Talk about the different sorts of balls and the marks they make. Which ones are best? Which ones make the best marks? Which ones are most difficult to use and why?

Ready for more...

▶ Try working in pairs, one rolling, the other catching, with the same ball or one each and different colours of paint.

▶ Try dropping some sponge balls full of paint on big pieces of paper for splatterball pictures.

▶ Put a ball inside a sock or a cut-off leg of tights, dip in paint and bounce along a piece of paper or even splat it against a piece of paper pinned on the wall. This is better done outside as it is messy!

▶ Cleaning up after these activities is part of the fun – use a big bowl of soapy water, a hose, or just tip the balls into the water tray and look at what happens as they swish around.

Marble marks

Rolling painty marbles in a tray encourages concentration as well as refining fine motor skills and hand/eye co-ordination.

What you need

- ▶ a shallow tray
- ▶ paint (not too thick); paper; scissors
- ▶ marbles or big round beads

What you do

Preparation

▶ Help the children to collect the equipment you need, and mix the paint. Let them choose the colours they would like to use. Help them to cut some paper to fit in the bottom of the tray.

Exploration

▶ The children can squirt, pour or spoon paint into the middle of the tray, choosing the colours they want.

▶ Then let them choose some marbles or beads to roll in the tray.

▶ As they tip the tray, the beads or marbles will roll through the paint, leaving tracks across the paper. Add more paint if needed.

Some extensions:

1. Limit the colours to seasonal tones or a range of shades of one colour.

2. Try the same method with toy cars or trucks.

Ready for more...

▶ Use a mixture of big and small beads and see what happens.

▶ Get a paddling pool and try the same idea with bigger balls and paint. It will probably need several children to rock the pool and make the balls move.

▶ Ride on trikes or bikes (or even a skateboard) through puddles of paint and onto long sheets of lining paper or wallpaper.

▶ Get some foil dishes and make holes in the bottom with a pencil. Put paint in the dish and drizzle the paint over sheets of paper. You could use a foil turkey roasting dish for a bigger area to drizzle paint on to.

▶ Line your slide with paper, put a tray at the bottom and roll painty balls or beads (or just painty drips) down the slide for longer trails and patterns.

String painting

The magic of these symmetrical patterns will fascinate some children. They are simple to do and can be offered as a totally independent activity.

What you need

▶ paper; paint in shallow dishes
▶ lengths of string (try different sorts and thicknesses)

What you do

Preparation

▶ Put the paint in shallow trays such as polystyrene or plastic food trays. Leave these and the string and paper so children can help themselves. Most children will already know what to do, some may need help from you or another child, or to watch for a while before getting involved.

Exploration

▶ The children need to dip a piece of string in the paint, then trail it on the paper so it leaves a trail. They can then use a different piece of string, with a different colour or thickness.

▶ Let the children have plenty of time to explore the different sorts of string and different sizes of paper.

▶ Take photos and talk with them about what they are doing.

An extension:

To make a string pattern or print, put a piece of string dipped in paint on the paper, fold the paper over the string, pat it down, then hold the paper with one hand as they pull the string out with the other. This takes co-ordination! You may need to help, but wait to be invited!

Ready for more...

▶ Try with several pieces of string of different colours, types or lengths.

▶ Offer some fluffy wool, ribbon, twine, lace, or fine rope as alternatives.

▶ Get some thin chain (bath plug chain from a plumber's works well). Dip this in paint and use it to trail around or make prints.

▶ Put on wellies and aprons and go outside. Stand in the middle of a big piece of paper or card and trail a 'painty' rope, dressing gown cord or chain around you, making a pattern on the paper. Tying knots in the rope makes it more interesting, and tassels make it even better!

Crinkly cellophane

Cellophane is a very different surface for mark making, producing transparent pictures and unusual effects.

What you need

- a selection of coloured or plain cellophane or gels
- poster or 'ready mixed' paint – pearlised paint works particularly well
- PVA or white glue
- fine paint brushes and cotton buds

What you do

Preparation

▶ Let the children help to mix paints with white glue in small containers, this will help the paint to stick to the cellophane. Try to offer some different colours, such as silver, gold, bronze or copper for a really shimmering effect.

Exploration

▶ Encourage children to experiment with the paints and their fingers on small pieces of cellophane. Use masking tape to stick the cellophane down if it is too slippery!

Some extensions:

1. Encourage the children to use a different finger for each colour – this will concentrate their minds and their muscles!

2. Talk about the colours and how they change when painted onto different colours of cellophane.

3. Begin to use words such as 'transparent' and new colours such as 'bronze'.

Ready for more...

▶ Offer some glitter in shakers or sequins to decorate the shiny pictures.

▶ Try working as a group on a very big sheet of cellophane or plastic sheeting.

▶ When dry, the children's work can be slipped into clear plastic sleeves for display.

▶ Groups of finished work or bigger creations can be displayed on a washing line, against a window or with a string of fairy lights behind to accentuate the colours.

▶ Set the cellophane into frames or the fronts of greetings cards.

▶ Try writing names or words for a new sort of word display.

▶ Mount different colours on top of each other to explore colour changes.

▶ Make some magic glasses with cellophane lenses.

Shiny surfaces

Painting on reflective, shiny, slippery surfaces is very different. Try some shiny surface painting to explore more things that marks can do.

What you need

▶ mirrors, mirror tiles, CDs, mirror sheet, foil card and plastic backed foil sheets

▶ paints

▶ PVA 'white' glue

▶ small mark makers such as fine brushes, cotton buds and twigs

SAFETY

Try to get safety mirrors, plastic mirrors or paint on metal surfaces.

What you do

Preparation
▶ This activity doesn't need much preparation, just offer the shiny surfaces and some paint mixed with PVA glue (the glue makes the paint stick better to the shiny surfaces).

Exploration
▶ Sit with the children as they work and talk about what they are doing. Look at the different sorts of foils and shiny surfaces. Explore how the light reflects in the objects and how reflections are distorted by different surfaces and movements.

▶ This sort of mark making is more complex and needs concentration. The surface is slippery as well as shiny, so some children may not like it. Watch for the children who can concentrate and persevere, and give more support to those who find it less rewarding.

Some extensions:
1. Do this activity outside where there is plenty of light, but NOT in bright sunshine because of the damage reflections may do to children's eyes.

2. Take some photos together to talk about later.

3. Encourage the children to explore different mark makers and their fingers.

Ready for more...

▶ Add more mark makers, such as pipe cleaners, pegs, toothbrushes.

▶ Encourage children to drip the paint in drops on the surface of the mirrors.

▶ Prop a safety mirror up securely and let children paint their own reflected faces – adding red noses, different coloured eyes, hats and big ears. Take photos of the mirror portraits for a 'Guess who this is?' display, before cleaning the paint off with soapy water.

▶ Put a mirror or shiny surface flat on the ground and let the children paint the clouds, trees or other objects they can see.

▶ Paint some old CDs and hang them up outside in trees or bushes, or make a mobile for the room by hanging them from threads on coat hangers or a dowell. Or to cover a whole wall!

▶ Use gold and silver paint on a long sheet of foil paper and use it as a hanging or room divider in your room. Add some feathers, sequins and other shiny bits.

Icing sugar patterns

A simple mixture of icing sugar and water will react with colours to make the brightest, prettiest marks on paper.

What you need

- ▶ a box of icing sugar, water for mixing and a thick paintbrush
- ▶ plain paper (white is best)
- ▶ small brushes, droppers or straws
- ▶ water based inks, food colouring or thin paint

What you do

Preparation

▶ Help the children to make the icing sugar mixture, adding five heaped teaspoons of icing sugar to about 125ml of water. Mix till the icing sugar has dissolved. Talk about what has happened to the sugar.

▶ Put ink, food colouring or thin paint in small containers, with thin brushes, straws or droppers nearby.

Exploration

▶ Using a wide paintbrush, help the children to spread the sugar mixture all over sheets of white paper.

▶ Now, with a brush, dropper or straw, drip ink, food colouring or thin paint onto the wet sugary paper. Watch the colour spread to create fantastic patterns!

Some extensions:

1. Get some bright fluorescent colours. These work really well!

2. Try mixing colours or dropping one colour inside another.

3. Talk about the reactions as the colour spreads, modelling and extending descriptive language about the activity.

Ready for more...

Remember that these creations will take some time to dry – encourage the children to be patient!

▶ Lay a long sheet of lining paper down a row of tables and work together to produce a collaborative pattern.

▶ Use a restricted range of colours or shades to make seasonal or topic linked patterns.

▶ Use the finished patterns to display photos, make cards or back display boards.

▶ Try other papers to see if the technique works on tissue, card, greaseproof paper, black or dark colours, paper towels, kitchen roll etc.

▶ Try the method on a table top or in a big shallow tray and take some prints of the patterns the children make.

▶ Take some photos during the process, as the patterns develop and change.

Vegetable printing

Familiar shapes of fruit and vegetables make lovely marks on paper. They are also good for making repeated patterns.

What you need

> fruit or vegtables – apples, carrots, potatoes, onions and oranges (ask a local greengrocer for ones that have gone past their sell-by date)
> knives (older children can cut their own fruit and vegetables) and forks
> paint in shallow trays
> lots of newspaper

What you do

Preparation and Exploration

▶ Look at the fruit and vegetables together, then help the children to cut some in half. If you stick a fork in the object to hold it steady while cutting, it will reduce the risk of the knife slipping!

▶ Look carefully at the insides of the cut vegetables and fruit, and talk about the sorts of patterns and prints each one might make.

▶ Put a thick layer of newspapers on the table (this will make a better bed for printing) and place a piece of clean paper on top. Put some paint in shallow containers.

▶ Let the children explore the fruit and vegetables by dipping them in the paint and printing with them.

Some extensions:

1. You may want to offer brushes for the paint, so it is not so thick on the printer.

2. A thin sponge in the bottom of the paint tray may help too.

3. Talk about the prints, looking at the object and the print it makes.

4. Take photos as the children work.

Ready for more...

▶ Potatoes are the cheapest vegetables to use, and you could help the children to cut some patterns and shapes in the surface of the cut halves, so they have plenty of different shapes to print with.

▶ Remember to cut some fruit and veg vertically as well as horizontally, or cut in chunks or quarters.

▶ Try star fruit, lemons, brussel sprouts, broccoli for a change. You could even cut a cabbage in half.

▶ Print with natural objects such as leaves, flowers, seed heads, stones, bark, moss, shells.

Bubbles

Children love bubbles, and taking prints from piles of bubbles you have blown yourself never loses its appeal.

What you need

- good quality washing-up liquid
- paint pots, plastic mugs or plastic soup containers
- paper or thin card and paint
- plastic drinking straws

I will need

SAFETY
Use a clean straw for each child to prevent the spread of infection.

!

What you do

Preparation

▶ Collect the resources and mix some fairly thin paint in plastic containers. Let the children put a squirt of washing-up liquid into each pot of paint and mix it up. Cut a little nick in each straw, about 2-3cm from the end – this will stop children sucking the paint by mistake!

Exploration

▶ Give the children plenty of time to blow through their own individual straw into the paint pots, until they have raised a pile of bubbles above the top of the pot.

▶ Children can make the bubble prints themselves by putting a piece of paper on top of the pile of bubbles.

Some extensions:

1. Talk about what happens to the bubbles as they blow, and after they have taken the print.

2. Try making prints with two different colours, by blowing and printing in two different paint containers and printing twice on the same paper.

Ready for more...

▶ Try using little hand whisks to make the bubbles.

▶ Make a bowl full of bubble mixture and let two or three children make the bubbles by using hand-held or rotary whisks until the bubbles rise above the bowl. Then use a bigger piece of paper, sharing the holding, to make a big bubble print.

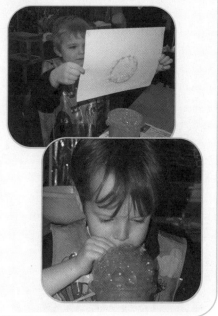

▶ Colour bubble mixture with food colouring, and use this with bubble blowers. Blow the bubbles and let them float down onto sheets of paper, where they will burst to leave patterns of colour.

▶ Sprinkle sheets of paper with a thin layer of powder paint. Blow clear or coloured bubbles above the sheet and when they land and pop, they will fix some of the paint with water.

Cracked Wax

Crayons and a strong pair of hands are all you need for this way of using colour and paint together.

What you need

- ▶ wax crayons
- ▶ strong paper
- ▶ a decorator's brush and dark paint (not too thick)
- ▶ kitchen roll

What you do

Preparation

▶ Collect the things you need, and talk with the children about what you are going to make. You could have a finished creation to show if you think you need it.

Exploration

▶ Encourage the children to draw a picture or make a pattern on a piece of paper. They need to press hard with the crayons and cover as much of the paper as possible. Blocks of colour are specially effective in this technique.

▶ Take some photos of the finished pictures and patterns for a 'before and after' comparison.

▶ Now get the children to crumple their pictures into a small ball, the smaller the better. This is to crack the wax.

▶ Flatten out the paper, and then cover the whole paper with watery paint, using a decorator's brush.

▶ Use some kitchen roll to gently dab off any excess paint to reveal a batik effect picture.

Ready for more...

▶ Iron the pictures with a cool iron between two sheets of paper (adult only).

▶ Coat the picture with a thin layer of dilute PVA glue to make a shiny surface.

▶ Make magic pictures by drawing with white candles or crayons on white paper, then painting over with thin paint to reveal the picture. Older children might like to make magic letters and messages this way too.

▶ Melt your crayon ends in a microwave or a low heat oven, then pour the wax into small containers to make new chunky crayons for use on big surfaces. Keep the colours separate or they will all turn out brown! This is an adult-only activity!

All sorts of paint!

More ideas for drawing and painting to try in your setting.

Help the children to make prints of their paintings   Mix the colours

Paint in drips and drops   Use both hands   Thin paint in spray bottles

Use painty sponges for hand printing

Roll a ball

Paint a CD

Paint with cotton buds

Isolate a finger

Use mud

Share an easel

Use a stick as a brush

Use your other hand

Be outside

Marbling

These floating inks make fascinating and unpredictable marks on paper. They were originally used to make endpapers for expensive books.

What you need

- ▶ a shallow tray, half filled with water
- ▶ marbling inks
- ▶ paper cut slightly smaller than the size of the tray

What you do

Preparation

▶ Talk with the children about how these inks work, and demonstrate if you think they need it.

▶ Half fill the tray with water.

Exploration

▶ Let the children drip the inks on the surface of the water, watching to see how the inks move around as they float.

▶ When they are happy with their ink pattern, help the child to carefully place a piece of paper on the surface of the water, over the ink pattern.

▶ Lift the paper carefully off the water and put it somewhere flat to dry. The paper will be covered with wonderful streaky patterns.

Some extensions:

1. Try gently mixing the inks together with a straw or the handle of a paintbrush to see what happens to the pattern.

2. Experiment with swirls and circles, lines and dots.

Ready for more...

▶ Use the papers to make wrapping paper, backgrounds for displays, sky for black paper silhouettes.

▶ Try to find some books with marbled endpapers, and then use your own marbled papers to make some book covers for your own story books or sketchbooks.

▶ Look up 'marbling' on Google Images for lots of examples of marbled papers to look at and download.

▶ You could do some 'real' marbling by mixing cooking oil with inks and floating this mixture on water. The finished prints will have a transparent look that is very attractive. Make sure children's clothing is well protected from the oily mixtures, as they may stain.

Bleach patterns

Dilute bleach works well on coloured paper. It's like magic when it removes the colour as you watch.

What you need

- ▶ tissue paper or crepe paper (darker colours work best)
- ▶ dilute bleach solution
- ▶ fine paintbrushes
- ▶ newspapers

SAFETY
Supervise the use of bleach, and don't use it with younger children.

What you do

Preparation

▶ Mix a dilute mixture of bleach and water. This is an adult task and should be done when children are NOT present in case the concentrated bleach spills. Different bleaches vary in strength, so practise with different strengths before using, and use the weakest solution you can. You should also make sure the children are well protected, with sleeves rolled up when they do the activity. Despite this, we feel this is a useful activity and the dilute bleach does not present a significant risk for older children in the Early Years Foundation Stage.

Exploration

▶ Let the children explore the mixture by dripping and painting it on paper shapes. The bleach will have an almost instant effect on the colours in the paper. Exploring this medium should be done in a one-to-one situation with an adult present.

An extension:

Take time to watch and talk about what happens as the colour disappears and the pattern or picture appears.

Ready for more...

▶ Black tissue works very well and gives quite startling results.

▶ For a good background for a window or a winter picture, try dropping bleach from droppers onto big sheets of black tissue and leaving the paper to dry. When displayed against a window, you will have a starry pattern.

▶ Try folding sheets or circles of tissue and dipping the edges into a shallow dish of bleach solution. Leave to dry, then unfold to find patterns like flowers or geometrical designs.

Weaving and tying

Weaving and tying help with finger, hand and wrist control, everyone can do it, and the results are often fabulous!

What you need

- garden trellis, plastic fencing or netting with large holes
- supports to tie it to – table legs, cupboards, door frames and climbing frames
- ribbon, string, cord, lace or fabric strips, various lengths and types

What you do

Preparation
▶ Make sure the netting or fence is securely fastened and stable – some children may use it to pull themselves up from kneeling or sitting, or may lean against it! Make sure the netting is taught, so children can see and work easily. Try to make it accessible from both sides.

Exploration
▶ Leave a basket of ribbons and other fabrics to tie and weave through the netting. The children can access this at any time during the day.

▶ You may need to show children how to knot and weave, but most children seem to know instinctively how to do it.

Some extensions:
1. Add fence and net weaving to your outdoor area as a child-initiated activity.

2. Talk about different sorts of knots and ways of fixing.

3. Encourage the children to take photos.

Ready for more...

▶ Cut coloured plastic carrier bags into strips and use these for waterproof outdoor weaving.

▶ Make a celebration hanging with gift ribbon, tinsel, shiny paper and sparkly fabrics.

▶ Weave with grasses, feathers, leaves and bendy twigs.

▶ Tie ribbons to the top of your climbing frame or the fence and watch them blow in the wind.

▶ Use crates, baskets, old fireguards, gates and fences for weaving and tying.

▶ Experiment with plaiting and twisting two or three ribbons or strips.

▶ Cut up old clothes or sheets into strips to recycle the fabric, unpick knitted garments, reuse wrapping paper – ask friends, parents, colleagues for donations of clean fabrics to use.

Tie dye

This activity is wonderful for strengthening hands and fingers, using the muscles later needed for writing. It's also a magical experience!

What you need

- an old bed sheet, preferably white or a pastel colour
- a packet of machine dye and some salt
- strong pegs, elastic bands and bulldog clips
- plastic toys and small objects (washing machine safe)
- access to a washing machine

What you do

Preparation

▶ You may want to make a trial tie dye piece by showing children the process of tying objects, then dipping them in dilute food colouring or paint.

▶ Collect the objects for tying – plastic pieces from constructions sets (Lego, Mobilo, Stickle Bricks etc) and buttons, beads, pebbles, small plastic toys; and plenty of bands, clips and pegs.

Exploration

▶ Before you make a big tie dye, let children experiment with small pieces of fabric, tying objects and clipping folds, then dipping them in paint or food colouring and leaving to dry before untying the objects to reveal the pattern.

Some extensions:

1. Suggest to the children that they might like to be involved in making a really big tie dye pattern on a bedsheet.

2. Start work with volunteers, and others will surely join in! Don't try to do this project over a short session – it may take a week or more to get enough objects tied in and all the children involved.

3. Show the children how to fold or scrunch the fabric, or wrap an object and fix it with elastic bands, pegs or clips. You can use more than one band to make several circles (see photo on page 64). The good thing about this method is that every child can be involved and those who are most interested can do more!

4. When the sheet can't take any more objects, check the bands are tight, put it in the washing machine and dye it according to the instructions on the packet.

5. Let the children help to unwrap the objects and reveal their pattern.

Ready for more...

▶ When the sheet is dry, use it for display, a tablecloth for snack time, curtains for the home corner, a cover for the climbing frame or a unique tent.

▶ One of these sheets will not be enough! Make some more – one for each season in seasonal colours, themed ones for the seaside or for story backgrounds.

More weaving and tying

The process in action!

Milk crates

Plastic covered netting

On the fence!

Net suspended from the ceiling, weighted at the bottom

Little plastic baskets (try peg baskets)

Wrapping a crate

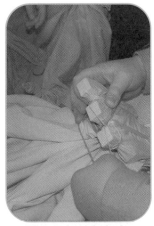

Wrapping and tying aid concentration

Elastic bands help

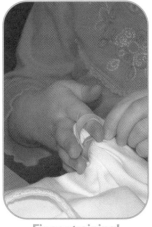

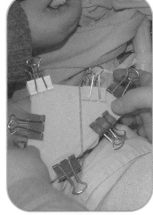

Finger training!

Clips of all colours

Wind it tight!

Use more than one band

Work together

All done!

Squash, squeeze, poke

The group of malleable materials which includes clay, dough and plasticene can all be used as surfaces for mark making.

What you need

▶ play dough (bought or made), natural clay, plasticene, air-drying clay, DAS Pronto, Milliput, Modelight, Fimo, Modair, or even pastry!

▶ tools, rolling pins and cutters

What you do

Preparation
▶ Collect the tools and materials. Make these available to the children at all times.

▶ It's better to start with malleable materials that don't dry out. These include natural clay and home-made doughs of all sorts. These are much more suitable for younger children to explore.

Exploration
▶ Give plenty of time for free play with these materials. Children may need to just play with them before rolling them out or making marks in them.

Some extensions:
1. Offer the rolling pins and mark makers and let the children experiment with them, rolling out the materials and trying all sorts of marks and patterns with cutters, stampers and objects.

2. As the children get used to working with malleable materials, they may want to keep what they make. This is the time to start introducing self-hardening types, explaining that they do dry out and then can't be changed.

Ready for more...

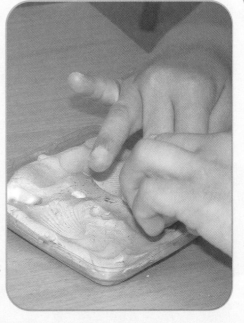

▶ Try pressing the material into shallow trays, pressing objects into the surface, then tipping it out so you get a small plaque.

▶ Offer some finer marking tools, such as old pencils, plastic cutlery, twigs and sticks so they can make finer patterns and draw pictures.

▶ Collect some natural materials such as feathers, shells, seeds and stones to mark the surfaces.

▶ Expand the use of this technique by encouraging 3D constructions where children cut and add pieces of clay etc to flat bases.
Try rolling a flat piece of clay, marking the surface, then rolling it into a cylinder round a cup or jar, so it stands up when the support is taken out.

Malleable marks

Printing with everyday objects will be familiar to all practitioners. Try some of these variations for some new mark making fun.

What you need

- ▶ a collection of small objects
- ▶ thin sponges, and shallow trays
- ▶ clay or plasticene, boards and rollers
- ▶ water based printing inks and small rollers (optional)

What you do

Preparation

▶ Collect a good selection of objects to press into clay or plasticene (spools, Lego bricks, coins, buttons, small word people, shells, nuts, pasta, stones, jewellery, beads etc). Put these where children can use them.

▶ Find rollers and boards, and clay or plasticene.

Exploration

▶ Give plenty of time for free play with the resources. Children can have a great deal of fun just rolling, pressing the objects in and rolling out again. This is all good for muscles of fingers and hands.

An extension:

Try making some simple printing blocks with plasticene. Make a ball of the material and press an object into it. Turn the ball over and use it to print with. It won't last long, as the pressure of their hands will squash the imprint, so the children will need to make a new one frequently. Wash each one and use new material while it dries.

Ready for more...

▶ Show the children how to form 'handles' for their printers by shaping the top of the material into a lump or ridge for their fingers before they press an obejct into the base.
This technique may be too hard for the younger ones.

▶ Use pieces of folded fabric to hold printing blocks or objects (see photo).

▶ Use pencils or plastic tools to make marks in pieces of polystyrene or food trays, then use these as printing blocks.

▶ Try some unusual objects such as shoes or kitchen implements to make prints with or to make printing blocks.

▶ As children become more used to making printing blocks, try using printing ink (water based kinds) and print rollers to cover the print block, then press it down on paper (put a thick layer of newspaper under the printing paper for a better print).

Clay drawing

This unusual way of using clay helps fine motor skills and children love it!.

What you need

- ▶ clay in one or more colours
- ▶ perspex or thin plastic (an empty laminating pouch is ideal)
- ▶ masking tape (children can use this unaided)
- ▶ simple line drawings

What you do

Preparation

▶ The line drawings can be ones drawn by children or adults, or tracings of pictures, possibly linked with your current topic or interests of the children.

▶ Provide all the things children need and show them how to stick the picture down if they need help.

Exploration

▶ Let the children choose a picture, put it under the plastic sheet and fasten this to the table.

▶ Now let them use the clay in any way they like to follow the line of the drawing. Some may use bits, some may make 'snakes' or little balls.

▶ When they have finished, they can gently slide the picture out and see their creation.

Ready for more...

▶ Make sure you take photos, as these pictures are not very robust!

▶ Try putting flattish things such as leaves, feathers or 2D shapes under the perspex.

▶ Make wool patterns under the plastic and let the children follow your pattern with their clay pieces.

▶ Draw spider webs, spirals and other patterns with straight and curved lines to follow.

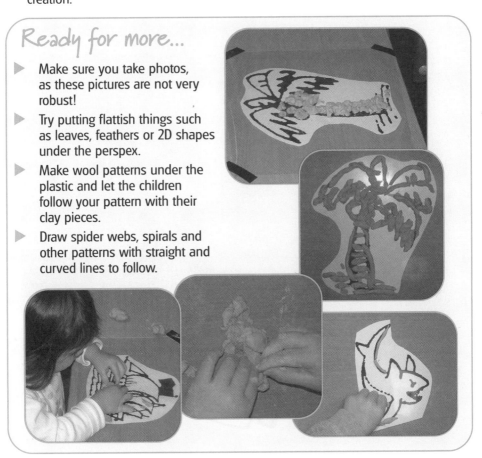

Magnets

Magnets are magical things, and these are even more magical to make marks with on a big surface such as a fridge door.

What you need

- sets of magnets and magnetic shapes (see end of book for suppliers)
- a large metal sheet, metal shelf, tray or a door from an old fridge or freezer
- small magnet boards or shallow baking trays

What you do

Preparation

▶ None.

Exploration

▶ Children of all ages love magents and magnetic toys and games. They will need no encouragement to get involved with these resources, which are easy for even the youngest or most insecure child to manipulate. The results are always good!

Some extensions:

1. Use part sets or sort the magnets into types, using only one type or colour.

2. Make repeating patterns, pictures or designs.

3. Let the children photograph these short lived creations.

4. Talk about how magnets work and see if they can find other places in your setting to make magnet creations.

Ready for more...

▶ Offer strings, ribbons and threads to wind in and out of the magnets.

▶ Suggest 'trapping' small pieces of coloured paper or magazine pictures under the magnets to make stories or scenes. These could be cut by the children and have drawings on.

▶ Link magnets together by tying strings between them or making paths with paper strips.

▶ Experiment with incorporating other metal objects such as washers, nails or small chains.

Polystyrene pins

Push pins come in many sizes and colours. They encourage fine motor skills and creativity in one activity. Get them from office supply stores or art shops.

What you need

▶ pieces of polystyrene or thick, firm sponge from packaging, or polystyrene tiles

▶ push pins

▶ thread, wool, ribbon, thin strips of fabric

SAFETY
Children need to be taught how to use these materials safely.

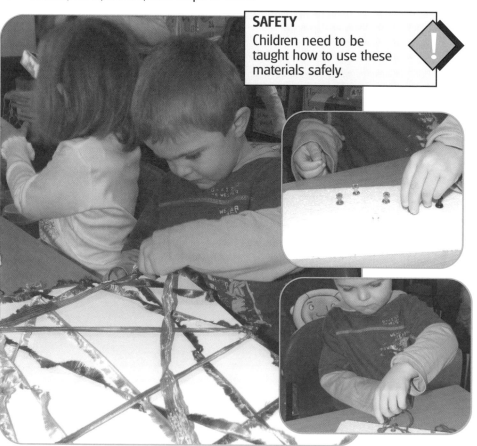

What you do

Preparation
▶ Teach the children how to use the pins safely. Once you have done this, collect together some strings and other decorative materials and arrange them for easy access.

Exploration
▶ Give the children time to explore the pins and polystyrene – some children may just enjoy pushing and removing the pins randomly, others will become fascinated by making patterns.

▶ Let them explore freely, just watch and listen.

Some extensions:
1. Offer the strings and things, and suggest that they could take a string or piece of wool for a walk from pin to pin.

2. Use a spare pin to secure the end of the string or ribbon.

3. This is a simple activity, but until children are familiar with the pins, make sure you supervise them carefully. This activity is not suitable for children who still put things in their mouths!

Ready for more...

▶ Try using cork tiles instead of polystyrene.
▶ Use a very big piece of polystyrene (like the base packaging from a TV or washing machine) for a group activity.
▶ For less skilled or younger children, offer polystyrene, tough foam or card from double-walled cardboard cartons with old ballpoint pens, pencils or other safe pointed tools so they can make punched patterns.

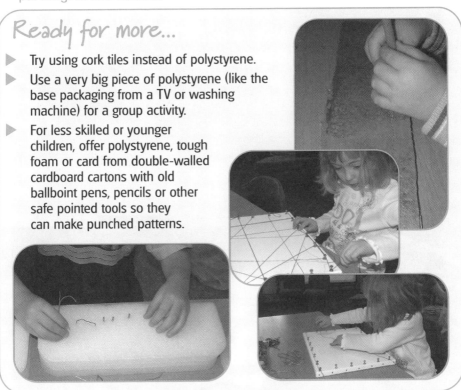

Writing in role

Role play is often the first place where children begin to make purposeful marks on surfaces. Exploit this by encouraging writing in all sorts of role play.

What you need

- pens, pencils, crayons, highlighter pens, felt pens
- staplers, hole punches, clipboards, whiteboards, telephones, keyboards
- diaries, notebooks, message pads, Post-its, shopping lists, order forms, carbon pads, calendars, envelopes, cards and notelets

What you do

Preparation

▶ Mark making and writing resources should be available in every role play situation, both indoors and outside. Plan this and build it in, then watch the children as they play in role, and add other things as the need arises.

▶ Store equipment where it is easily available and can be seen by the children. Make sure they have a choice of mark making tools and surfaces, and add some simple 'frames' such as shopping lists, diaries, recipes and order forms.

Exploration

▶ Children should meet these resources everywhere, indoors and outside. They may also need models of how to use them. You could sit near the children and model the use, or invite vistors to talk about what they do (prime them before the visit so they bring their notebooks, order forms, records, maps, plans etc to show the children). Look at books, watch videos and talk about what adults do in their daily lives. And don't forget to offer writing in home play situations.

An extension:

Each time you change your role play focus, ask the children what they know about the mark making associated with this activity – what do firemen, waiters, doctors, spacemen need?

Ready for more...

▶ As children become more experienced mark makers, offer a wider variety of ideas, such as vocabulary lists, plans and maps, message pads and notice boards, book making resources.

▶ Encourage children to take photos of their role play activities and make photo books or Powerpoint presentations.

▶ Use the interactive whiteboard or a computer to display children's photos or pictures to stimulate role play and real life writing activities.

▶ Look out for bargains in diaries, notelets, birthday cards, postcards, pens. Ask parents for unused cards, envelopes, diaries etc.

More role-play ideas

Make a shopping list

Order some bricks

Draw plans

Observe other people

Design a house

Write a diary

Make an appointment

Write a list

Do the register

What do we need?

Make a shop

Check the calendar

Go to the office

Label your drawing

Make a notice

Phone a friend

Take a message

Give a receipt

Patterns of light

Children love torches and the marks of light they make. Get different sorts and sizes from DIY stores or garages, including some wind-up varieties.

What you need

I will need

▶ a selection of torches – different sizes from mini to large, including some with coloured bulbs

▶ a dark area or a dark box or dark sheet

What you do

Preparation

▶ Collect the torches together and look at them with the children. turn off the lights and close curtains or blinds to start with, so children don't get frightened.

Exploration

▶ Give plenty of time for free play with the torches. Provide big boxes, pop-up tents, fabrics and pegs and other materials so children can make their own shelters independently or with your help.

▶ Talk about what is happening, what they are doing and the marks the torches make on surfaces.

Some extensions:

1. Add some music and see if the children are affected and move the torch beams to the music.

2. Talk about making wiggle snake beams, zigzags, shadows and spotlights.

3. Provide enough torches for children to use one in each hand to make beams that cross or follow each other.

Ready for more...

▶ If you haven't got a dark corner or space, make a 'dark box'. You could get a really big carton (from a fridge or washing machine) and cover it with dark paper or fabric inside and out so it shows the torch patterns. Hang dark material over the entrance as well. Hang or stick stars and shiny objects inside to catch the light.

▶ Make a 'dark wall' by pinning a black sheet on the wall and the floor nearby.

▶ Make up a dance or song about the lights, called 'Fireworks' or 'Fairy Dance' or 'Wiggly Worms' and accompany the dance or song with lights. On a winter afternoon, it might be dark enough to do this outside.

Interactive whiteboards

These pieces of equipment are becoming more common in settings – make sure they are used for child-initiated activities, not just teaching!

What you need

▶ an interactive whiteboard
▶ whiteboard software such as Colour Magic

What you do

Preparation

▶ Learn the possibilities of your whiteboard, and expand its use for children. Find out which programs are easy to access, and if you need to, ask for help from your ICT co-ordinator.

Exploration

▶ Using a whiteboard may be easier for some young children than trying to use a mouse and keyboard. Make sure the children know how to use the whiteboard as early as they can.

▶ Provide flexible, child friendly programs or free access during child-initiated time.

▶ Encourage children to experiment and praise their efforts. Let children teach each other! Make sure they know how to change the colour, line width, and tools for shapes and filling.

Ready for more...

▶ Encourage large movements with one or two markers, using the whole board.

▶ Use the programs on a computer if you don't have access to a whiteboard.

▶ Display photos on the whiteboard to inspire mark making and drawing.

▶ Offer objects for close observational drawing.

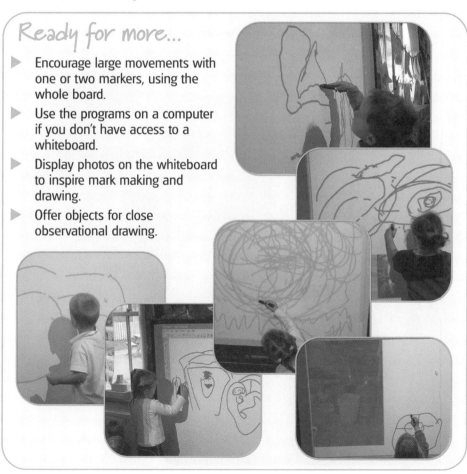

Photography

Every setting should have a digital camera, and every child should learn how to use it! When children record their own learning this becomes a powerful tool.

What you need

- ▶ child friendly cameras
- ▶ printer; laminator (optional)

What you do

Preparation
▶ Teach all the children how to use the camera safely, and make it available at all times. A neck strap is advisable to avoid accidental dropping.

Exploration
▶ The good thing about digital cameras is that the photos don't need to be developed, and children can experiment with different shots and sequences as well as capturing key experiences, vistors, their own work and that of their friends. Display children's photos prominently and add their names.

▶ Show children how to use the camera screen, the dock or link to the computer and the link to the whiteboard if you have one. This will enable them to become much more independent and confident photographers.

An extension:
1. You could sometimes appoint a group photographer to record some of the things that happen during a day. This will give a new and unique view of life in your setting and what the children think is important!

Ready for more...

▶ Suggest that the children photograph their favourite activity or place in your setting. Make a book of photos.

▶ Let children photograph each other for a portrait book or e-book.

▶ Make photographic labels for equipment and places.

▶ Collect photographs of role play characters or settings so you can remind children of places and people.

▶ Appoint a photographer when you go out on visits and walks. You may need more than one so nobody misses the fun or being in the photos.

▶ Take photos together of sequences of activities such as brick building, 'before' and 'after', plant growth, seasons changing in your garden, the growth of tadpoles, worms, slugs and snails, special occasions and other significant events, to remind children of what has happened and favourite memories.

Light boxes

Light boxes are a recent addition to early years settings, and they are expensive, but they are certainly fascinating for both adults and children.

What you need

▶ access to a light box
▶ transparent, translucent and opaque objects and papers

> **SAFETY**
> Supervise use of electrical equipment and make sure it is PAT tested.

You can see through transparent objects. Translucent objects let light through, so you can see shadows or outlines of objects behind them. Opaque objects do not let light through at all!

What you do

Preparation
▶ Leave the objects near the light box and switch it on.

Exploration
▶ Let the children have plenty of time to explore what the light box does and how it affects the objects they put on it.

▶ Take photos and talk with them about what happens.

An extension:
Continue to explore objects with the light box, ask open questions about them and talk about their properties.

Ready for more...

▶ Offer transparent gels and translucent papers and explore how colours change in overlapping pieces.

▶ Collect transparent and translucent objects that are all one colour or no colour. Experiment with these. Look for picnic glasses, plates and cutlery, plastic bowls and clear plastic jewellery, toys and other accessories, or jelly shoes, hair bands, hair clips.

▶ Find some plastic sheet, transparency film or transparent file pockets and draw on these with whiteboard or permanent markers. Put these on the light box and see what happens.

▶ Try ribbons, fabrics and items of clothing to explore their properties in light.

▶ Colour some water with food colouring and add cellulose paste to thicken it; or make some jelly; or use some coloured oils or marbling inks. Put these mixtures in transparent, sealed containers such as plastic food boxes, small screw topped plastic jars or zip-lock bags and look at these on the light table. Make sure the containers are leak-proof and supervise their use carefully.

Overhead projectors

This cheaper version of a light box is often available in schools or might be borrowed from your local school. It projects the image onto walls or a screen.

What you need

- an OHP machine
- a screen or clear, pale coloured wall or sheet to project onto
- objects to project, pens and OHP film

SAFETY

Supervise use of electrical equipment and make sure it is PAT tested.

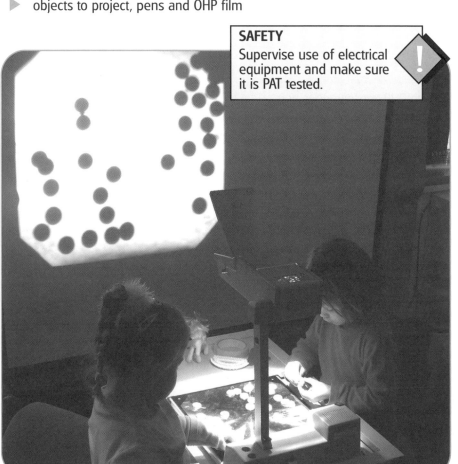

What you do

Preparation
▶ Teach the children how to use the OHP machine safely, including safe behaviour around plugs and cables. Tape cables to the floor. Collect a selection of objects to start the children off.

Exploration
▶ This piece of equipment is safe for children to use independently, but they should be aware that the bulb gets hot, and they should be within sight of an adult at all times.

▶ Let the children explore what the projector can do, including projecting their hands and arms, and even their whole bodies!

Some extensions:
1. Add some transparent objects (both coloured and clear).

2. Talk about what happens, using open questions and appropriate vocabulary.

Ready for more...

▶ Use OHP transparencies and OHP pens to draw and make other marks to show on the projector.

▶ Print some of their photos onto OHP transparencies (get the right sort or they may melt in your printer!).

▶ Cut out paper shapes and figures of objects, animals and people to make pictures and stories. Children can cut these from comics and magazines to make their own versions of favourite stories.

▶ Look at paper doileys and lacy fabrics on the projector and see how they look. Make snowflakes from paper and project them.

▶ Use the projector for counting and sorting small objects.

Some more ideas

Here are a few more ideas for mark making activities that you could introduce in your setting.

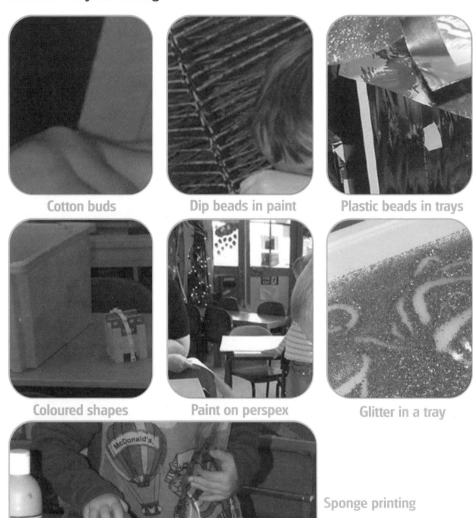

Cotton buds

Dip beads in paint

Plastic beads in trays

Coloured shapes

Paint on perspex

Glitter in a tray

Sponge printing

Tough foam and wire

Lids and coloured sticks

Lollipop sticks

Paint with mud

Draw in mud

Nails

Porridge oats

Splash painting

Tap-tap

What happened when a group of children started working with a pile of unwanted CDS and a big space!

Resources, websites and schemes for developing motor skills

Brain Gym Movements

'Brain Gym is a program of movements that enhance learning and performance in ALL areas. Brain Gym includes 26 easy and enjoyable activities that integrate body and mind to bring about rapid and often dramatic improvements in concentration, memory, reading, organizing, listening, physical co ordination and more'. Taken from **www.braingym.org/about.html**

Write Dance

Write Dance encourages a wide range of movements in a variety of ways and in a rhythmical manner to music. Across Europe the programme is widely used to introduce handwriting using music, movement and exercise. A specific programme for children aged 3-5 years is available.

Val Sabin's Activate

'The Activate with music programmes take whole classes of children through three dimensional repetitive movement activities within their personal space. Each activity is to music, which enables tempo and rhythm in the movements of the children to be varied through changes in the music.' Taken from **www.valsabinpublications.com/activate/index.htm** There are four levels of Activate, which will allow you to use the scheme with children up to Year 6!

Jabadeo

www.jabadao.org is the contact for the Centre for Movement Studies. Visit here for programmes, books and resources to help with movement, dance and rhythm, such as ribbon sticks and lycra.

The **Little Books** series consists of:

All Through the Year
Bags, Boxes & Trays
Bricks and Boxes
Celebrations
Christmas
Circle Time
Clay and Malleable Materials
Clothes and Fabrics
Colour, Shape and Number
Cooking from Stories
Cooking Together
Counting
Dance
Dance, with music CD
Discovery Bottles
Dough
50
Fine Motor Skills
Fun on a Shoestring
Games with Sounds
Growing Things
ICT
Investigations
Junk Music
Language Fun
Light and Shadow

Listening
Living Things
Look and Listen
Making Books and Cards
Making Poetry
Mark Making
Maths Activities
Maths from Stories
Maths Songs and Games
Messy Play
Music
Nursery Rhymes
Outdoor Play
Outside in All Weathers
Parachute Play
Persona Dolls
Phonics
Playground Games
Prop Boxes for Role Play
Props for Writing
Puppet Making
Puppets in Stories
Resistant Materials
Role Play
Sand and Water
Science through Art
Scissor Skills

Sewing and Weaving
Small World Play
Sound Ideas
Storyboards
Storytelling
Seasons
Time and Money
Time and Place
Treasure Baskets
Treasureboxes
Tuff Spot Activities
Washing Lines
Writing

All available from
www.acblack.com/featherstone